HOW TO DRAW™
SCOTLAND

D1396020

Robert the Bruce
statue, Bannockburn

Mark Bergin

BOOK  HOUSE

04288012

SALARIYA

Published in Great Britain in MMXIV by
Book House, an imprint of
The Salariya Book Company Ltd
25 Marlborough Place, Brighton BN1 1UB

1 3 5 7 9 8 6 4 2

Author: **Mark Bergin** was born in Hastings in 1961. He
studied at Eastbourne College of Art and has specialised in
historical reconstructions as well as aviation and maritime
subjects since 1983. He lives in Bexhill-on-Sea with his
wife and three children.

Editor: Stephen Haynes

PB ISBN: 978-1-909645-18-9

A CIP catalogue record for this
book is available from the
British Library.

Printed and bound in China.
Printed on paper from
sustainable sources.

**WARNING: Fixatives should be
used only under adult supervision.**

Visit our websites to read
interactive **free** web books, stay up
to date with new releases, catch
up with us on the
Book House Blog, view our
electronic catalogue and more!

www.salariya.com
Free electronic versions of four of
our You Wouldn't Want to Be titles

www.book-house.co.uk
Online catalogue
Information books
and graphic novels

www.scribobooks.com
Fiction books

www.scribblersbooks.com
Books for babies, toddlers and
preschool children

**www.flickr.com/photos/
salariyabookhouse**
View our photostream with sneak
previews of forthcoming titles

Join the conversation on Facebook
and Twitter by visiting
www.salariya.com

PAPER FROM
SUSTAINABLE
FORESTS

For **free** step-by-step tutorials
by Mark Bergin, visit our
YouTube channel at:
**www.youtube.com/user/
theSalariya**

Visit
www.salariya.com
for our online catalogue and
free interactive web books.

Contents

Making a start

Scotland has many fine subjects for the artist, such as landscapes, buildings and famous monuments. To get some ideas of drawing styles, you could visit art galleries, look at books or see how your friends draw — eventually you will develop your own way of seeing.

Robert the Bruce statue, Stirling

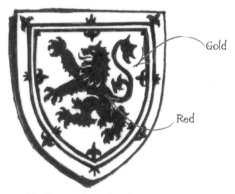

Gold

Red

Scottish royal coat of arms

Keep practising. If a drawing doesn't look good, start again. Keep working at it.

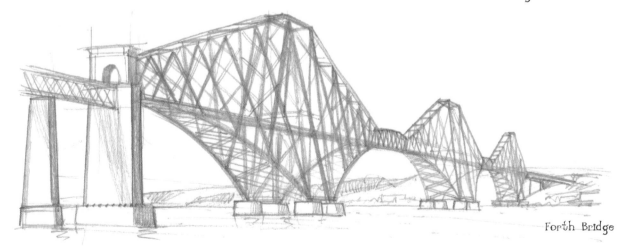

Forth Bridge

Look up close at real buildings and study the different textures of stones, bricks and wood.

Scott Monument, Edinburgh

If you are drawing an object near a lake, river or even a pond, remember to sketch in a faint reflection in the water.

Falkirk Wheel

Style and medium

There are many different materials you can draw with, such as pencil, ink, pastels or wax crayons. Experiment to see what works best for your chosen subject.

Drawing an outline in ink and colouring it in will make a silhouette.

The national flower of Scotland is the thistle.

Prehistoric village of Skara Brae, Orkney: pencil

Very dark shading shows recesses in the stonework.

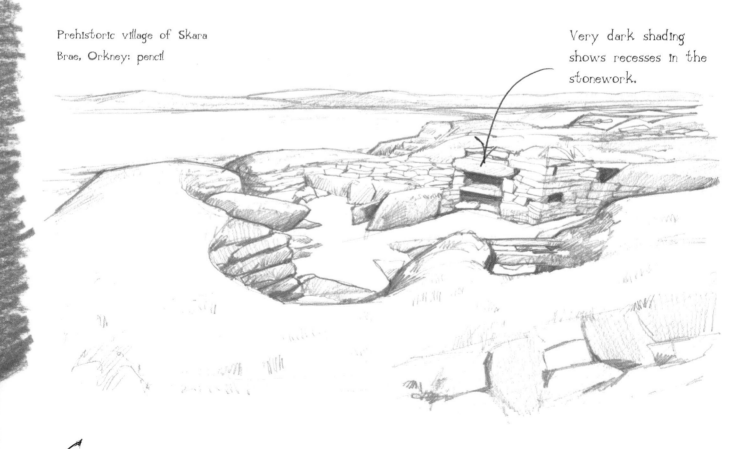

John Knox House,
Edinburgh: ink

Lines drawn in **ink** cannot be erased, so keep your ink drawings sketchy and less rigid. Don't worry about mistakes as these lines can be lost in the drawing as it develops.

Hard **pencils** are greyer and soft pencils are blacker. Hard pencils are usually graded from 6H (the hardest) through 5H, 4H, 3H and 2H to H. Soft pencils are graded from B, 2B, 3B, 4B and 5B up to 6B (the softest). The common HB pencil is between H and B.

Highland cows: coloured pencil

7

Perspective

If you look at any object from different viewpoints, you will see that the part that is closest to you looks larger, and the part furthest away from you looks smaller. Drawing in perspective uses this effect to create a feeling of depth — to show three dimensions on a flat surface.

Use basic construction lines to help you align each part of the drawing.

The vanishing point (V.P.) is the place in a perspective drawing where parallel lines appear to meet.

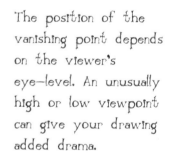

The position of the vanishing point depends on the viewer's eye-level. An unusually high or low viewpoint can give your drawing added drama.

Research ship *Discovery*, Dundee

Melrose Abbey

V.P. 2

V.P. 1 • —————————————— • V.P. 2

In two-point
perspective, the two
sides of the building
recede to separate
vanishing points on the
horizon line.

In the larger drawings
on this page, the left
vanishing point (V.P. 1)
is off the page, but
it's still useful to
know where it is.

V.P. 1 • —————————————— • V.P. 2

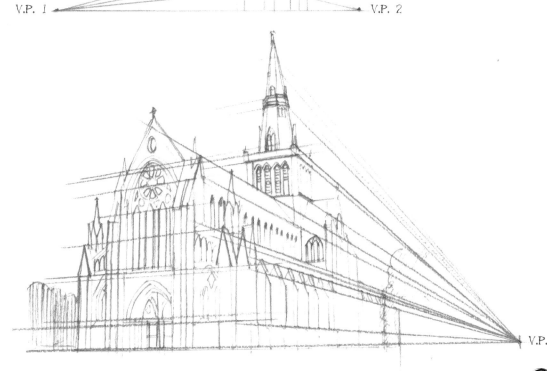

Glasgow Cathedral

V.P. 2

9

Using photographs

Drawing from photos can help you learn to draw shape and form more accurately.

Choose a good clear photograph and carefully trace it.

Draw a grid of squares over your tracing, then lightly draw another grid with the same number of squares on your drawing paper. If you wish, you can enlarge or reduce your drawing by changing the size of the squares. (Enlarging by this method is called **squaring up**.) Carefully copy the shapes from each square of the tracing paper onto your new grid.

Once the outline is complete, you can add more details to your drawing if you wish. Keep referring to the grid on your tracing to keep everything accurate.

You can add form to your drawing with shading. Decide which way the light is coming from, then add shadows to the parts that face away from the light.

Light source

Add more tone and detail to finish your drawing. It is up to you how much detail to include.

Glamis Castle, Angus

Holyrood Palace

Holyrood Palace in Edinburgh is the official residence of the Queen while she is in Scotland. It is said to be haunted by the ghost of Bald Agnes, executed for witchcraft in 1591.

Begin your drawing with a rectangle, with a line inside a little more than halfway up.

Try not to draw these construction lines in too heavily; you may want to erase them later.

Add another rectangle on either side for the wings of the building.

Loosely sketch in guidelines for the towers, roofs and ground-floor entrance.

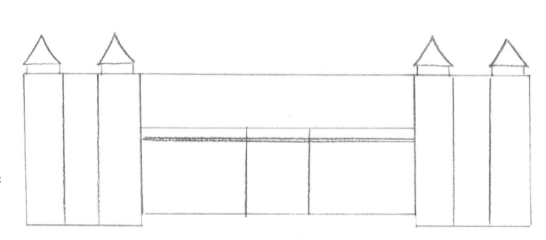

Start adding
details. Add the
pillars, chimneys and
crenellations.

Indicate where the
windows will go.

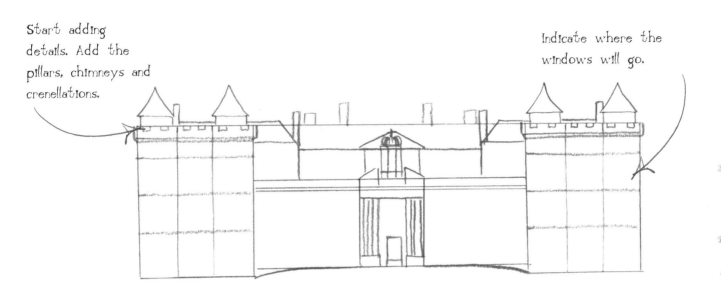

Add as much detail
as you like to the
windows and chimneys.

The door has a crest
above it and a sentry
box on either side.

Finish your drawing by
adding shading to the
building to give it a
sense of form.

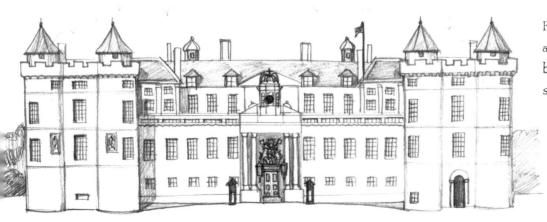

13

Wallace Monument

This 220-foot (67-metre) sandstone tower commemorating the 13th-century hero Sir William Wallace stands on Abbey Craig, near Stirling. Designed by the Edinburgh-born architect John Thomas Rochead, it was completed in 1869.

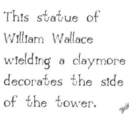

Start off by lightly sketching in the basic shapes of the building, including triangles for the roofs.

Add in the outlines of the stepped roof, the gateway and the base for the spires on the top of the tower.

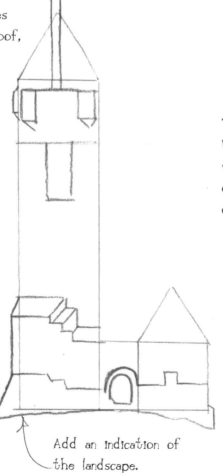

Add an indication of the landscape.

This statue of William Wallace wielding a claymore decorates the side of the tower.

14

Add guidelines for drawing the spiral staircase.

Start adding the intricate spires that decorate the top of the tower.

Draw the outbuilding with its stepped gable.

Add as much detail as you like.

Another view of the top of the tower.

Add foliage to give an indication of scenery.

Crown and sceptre

Officially called the Honours of Scotland, the Scottish crown jewels are the oldest set of crown jewels in the British Isles, dating from the 15th and 16th centuries.

Begin by drawing out the basic shape of the top, band and brim of the crown.

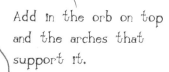

Add in the orb on top and the arches that support it.

Add the gold cross on top and the gold shapes that decorate the circlet.

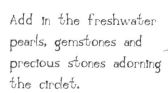

Add in the freshwater pearls, gemstones and precious stones adorning the circlet.

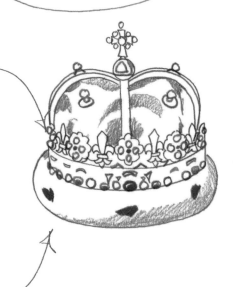

Add some texture to the velvet and ermine.

Shade the crown, leaving white highlights on the jewels to show how they shine.

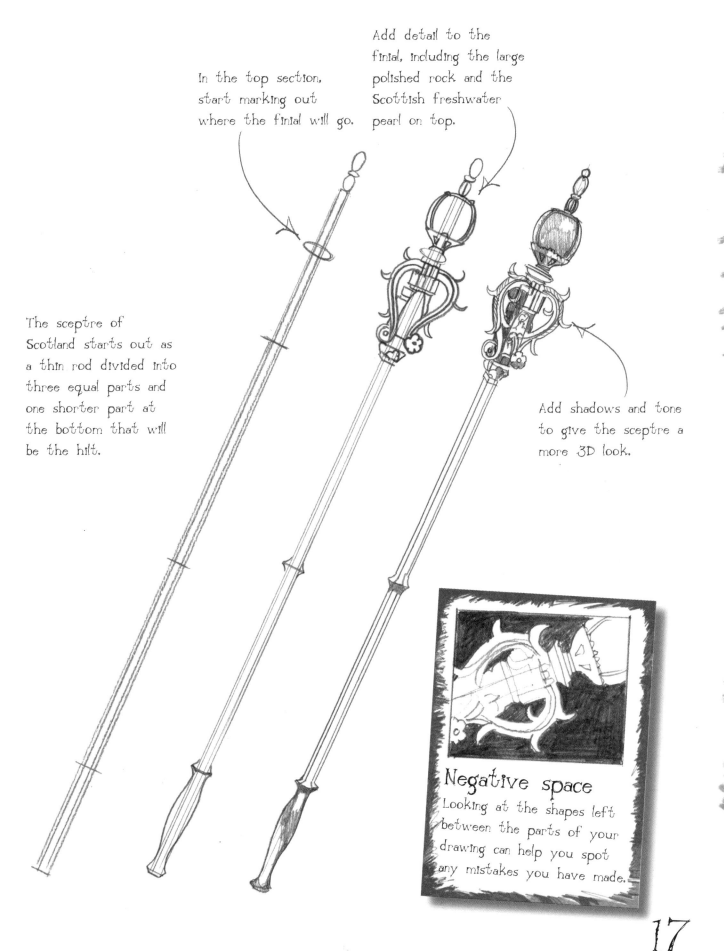

In the top section, start marking out where the finial will go.

Add detail to the finial, including the large polished rock and the Scottish freshwater pearl on top.

The sceptre of Scotland starts out as a thin rod divided into three equal parts and one shorter part at the bottom that will be the hilt.

Add shadows and tone to give the sceptre a more 3D look.

Negative space

Looking at the shapes left between the parts of your drawing can help you spot any mistakes you have made.

17

Highland piper

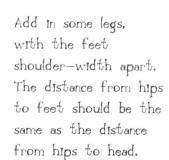

The Great Highland Bagpipe is known worldwide for its use in military and civilian bands, accompanied by different types of drummers.

Start with ovals for the piper's head, chest and hips.

Add in some legs, with the feet shoulder-width apart. The distance from hips to feet should be the same as the distance from hips to head.

Draw in the piper's neck, shoulders and arms. The left arm will be further away from the body to make room for the bag.

Start adding the
clothes and bagpipes.

Add details to the
pipes and costume, and
give the piper some
facial features.

Finish the piper's
clothing and add tone
and texture to give
him a 3D feel.

19

Highland dancer

Sword dancing originated as a preparation for warfare. It was a way of testing the warrior's agility and skill for the coming battle.

Begin by drawing ovals for the dancer's head, chest and hips. Note the tilt of the hips— this makes the pose more interesting.

Add legs. Make sure the right foot is directly under the centreline of the body, or the dancer will be off—balance.

Draw shoulders and arms. Put the left hand on the hip, with the right held above the head.

20

Start to add the basic shapes of the clothing. Put plenty of movement into the kilt.

Add more detail to the face, hands and hair. Put tartan detailing on the kilt and socks.

Using a mirror
Try looking at your drawing in a mirror. Seeing it in reverse can help you identify any mistakes.

Finish the drawing off with shading to add depth, and two crossed swords. This dance is called the Gillie Callum.

21

Balmoral Castle

Balmoral Castle in Aberdeenshire has been a private royal residence since it was built in 1856. The architect was William Smith, but Queen Victoria's husband, Prince Albert, also had a hand in the design.

Begin with a rectangular skeleton for the building.

Don't forget the shorter tower on the other side.

Add the main tower. Perspective will make the side wall appear to recede.

Add in the smaller turrets and crenellations to the towers.

Draw in the peaked
roofs and additional
crenellations on the
tops of the towers.
Add in the chimneys.

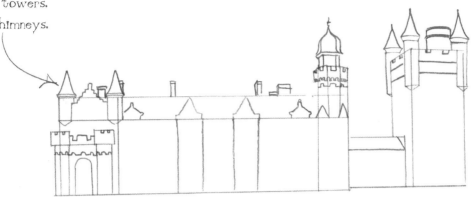

Add the windows and
final details such as
the flagpole.

Finish the drawing by
shading the building and
adding some foliage in
the background.

Eilean Donan

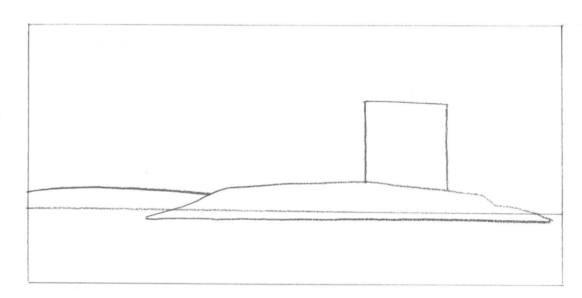

Eilean Donan is a tidal island in Loch Duich, in the western Highlands. The castle, ruined in the Jacobite risings of the 18th century, was rebuilt in the early 20th century.

Draw the island, the main tower of the castle and the top of the bridge that connects the island to the mainland.

Add shapes to indicate the outlying buildings and the slope of the hill.

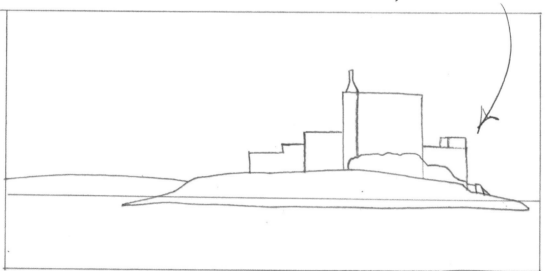

24

Add the arches of
the bridge, the trees
and the details of
the castle.

Add the hills in
the background.

Composition
Your drawing will look
quite different depending on
whether you place it in a
vertical or horizontal frame.

The light is coming from
the right in this drawing,
so the left-facing walls
are in shadow.

Ben Nevis

At 4,410 feet (1,344 metres) tall, Ben Nevis is the highest mountain in the British Isles.

Begin by sketching in the outlines of the mountain and surrounding foothills.

Choose a light source and add shadows to the sides facing away from the light. Add clouds to bring the background to life.

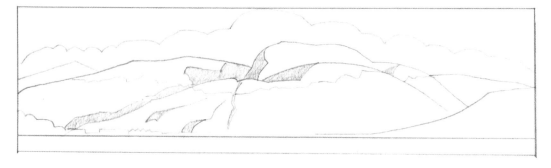

Add subtle texture to the sides of the mountain to indicate the scrub that grows there.

Loch Ness

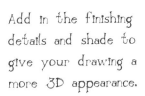

This vast, deep freshwater loch (lake) is most famous for reported sightings of the mythical Loch Ness Monster, or 'Nessie'.

Start with a horizontal line for the surface of the water.

Add in the hills and the basic shape of the building in the foreground.

Add Urquhart Castle in the centre, then add guidelines for the paths and walls.

Add in the finishing details and shade to give your drawing a more 3D appearance.

Edinburgh Castle

Edinburgh Castle is built on an extinct volcano, Castle Rock. There has been a royal castle on this site since the 12th century.

Lay down the hill and the outline of the castle walls.

Add more detail to the walls.

Atmospheric perspective

Because of the way light is scattered by the atmosphere, distant objects look paler and bluer than nearby objects.

28

Add the castle at the top of the hill and its surrounding walls.

Include some rugged texture on Castle Rock.

Choose a light source and add shadows to the sides facing away from it.

Atmospheric perspective (see opposite) makes objects in the foreground appear darker than those in the background.

29

V&A at Dundee

This exciting new museum of design, associated with London's Victoria & Albert Museum, is scheduled to be completed by 2016. The design is by the Japanese architect Kengo Kuma.

Draw a cuboid for the base. Remember, perspective will cause it to look smaller towards the back.

Take a triangle out of the side.

Slope the sides as shown to give the building its distinctive shape.

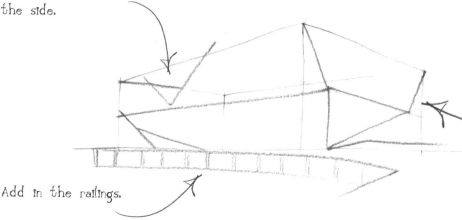

Add in the railings.

Add shading for depth and details to create interest, such as the reflection of the building in the water and the hint of buildings in the distance.

The tourist figure gives a sense of scale.

Scottish Parliament

The controversial Scottish Parliament Building in Edinburgh has won numerous architectural awards since its opening in 2004. The architect, Enric Miralles, died before the work was completed.

Lay out the basic shapes of the building in perspective.

Add in the canopy and the pillars that hold it up.

Add the details to the tops of the buildings and indications of where the windows will go.

Add the windows and as much detail as you like on the walls.

Add shading to give the building a 3D feel.

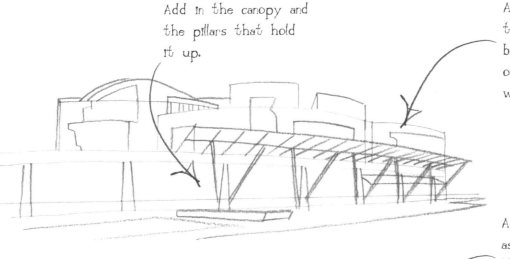

31

Glossary

Atmospheric perspective A method of showing depth in a landscape by making distant objects paler and bluer than near ones.

Composition The arrangement of the parts of a picture on the drawing paper.

Construction lines Guidelines used in the early stages of a drawing; they may be erased later.

Fixative A kind of resin sprayed over a drawing to prevent smudging. **It should only be used by an adult.**

Light source The direction from which the light seems to come in a drawing.

Perspective A method of drawing in which near objects are shown larger than faraway objects to give an impression of depth.

Proportion The correct relationship of scale between each part of the drawing.

Silhouette A drawing that shows only a flat dark shape, like a shadow.

Squaring up A method of creating an enlarged copy of a drawing or photograph using a grid of squares.

Vanishing point The place in a perspective drawing where lines that are really parallel appear to meet.

Index